Gods and Goddesses of Ancient Egypt

GODS AND GODDESSES
of Ancient
Egypt
Egyptian Mythology for Kids

MORGAN E. MORONEY

ILLUSTRATED BY MEEL TAMPHANON

ROCKRIDGE
PRESS

Interior and Cover Designer: Julie Gueraseva
Art Producer: Janice Ackerman
Editor: Laura Bryn Sisson
Production Editor: Jenna Dutton
Custom Illustration: © 2019 Meel Tamphanon

Interior Photography: pps: xii-xiii: Artindo/shutterstock.com; p.5: Purchase, Edward S. Harkness Gift, 1926/The Metropolitan Museum of Art; p. 19: Ewa Studio/shutterstock.com; p. 25: Marcelo Alex/shutterstock.com; p. 31: Funds from various donors, 1886 (86.1.14, .18, .21, .28) Gift of J. Lionberger Davis, 1967 (67.80)/The Metropolitan Museum of Art; p. 39: Ashwin/shutterstock.com; p. 45: Jaroslav Moravcik/shutterstock.com; p. 53:Kokhanchikov/shutterstock.com; p. 59: Theodore M. Davis Collection, Bequest of Theodore M. Davis, 1915/Metropolitan Museum of Art; p. 65: Rogers Fund, 1930/Metropolitan Museum of Art; p. 71: Mike P Shepherd / Alamy Stock Photo; p. 77: Gift of J. Pierpont Morgan, 1917/Metropolitan Museum of Art; p. 85: Pius Lee/shutterstock.com; p. 89: Harris Brisbane Dick Fund, 1956/The Metropolitan Museum of Art; p. 95: Gift of Pierpont Morgan, 1917/The Metropolitan Museum of Art; p. 105: Gift of Edward S. Harkness, 1921/The Metropolitan Museum of Art; p. 109: Rogers Fund, 1916/The Metropolitan Museum of Art; p. 115: Gift of Egypt Exploration Fund, 1901/The Metropolitan Museum of Art; p. 121: De Agostini Picture Library / S. Vannini / Bridgeman Images; p. 127: Marcelo Alex/shutterstock.com

ISBN: Print   978-1-64611-423-8
         eBook 978-1-64611-424-5

R0

For my family

CONTENTS

Introduction   viii

RA
The Sun God
1

SHU AND TEFNUT
God of Air and Goddess of Moisture
7

GEB AND NUT
God of the Earth and Goddess of the Sky
13

NEITH
Goddess of Creation and War
21

OSIRIS
God of the Underworld
27

ISIS
Goddess of Magic, Thrones, and Healing
33

HORUS THE CHILD AND HORUS THE ELDER
Child God of Healing and Falcon God of Kings
41

SETH
God of Deserts, Storms, War, and Chaos
47

NEPHTHYS AND THE FOUR SONS OF HORUS
Goddess of the Dead and Guardians of the Dead
55

ANUBIS
God of Mummification
61

SERQET
Goddess of Scorpions
67

HATHOR
Goddess of Love, Music, and Celebration
73

SEKHMET
Goddess of Power, War, and Plague
79

BASTET
Goddess of Cats, Joy, and Motherhood
85

PTAH
God of Craftsmen
91

THOTH
God of Knowledge, Writing, and Scribes
97

SESHAT
Goddess of Scribes, Building, and Astronomy
105

BES AND TAWERET
God and Goddess of Home, Childbirth, Women, and Children
111

SOBEK
God of Crocodiles and the Waters
117

KHNUM
God of Potters and the Flood
123

Family Tree of the Gods   128
Glossary   130
Find Out More   140
References   142

INTRODUCTION

The ancient Egyptians are remembered for their impressive accomplishments and for the power, richness, and longevity of their civilization—nearly 3,500 years! They built huge pyramids, created beautiful art, established an empire, and made mummies and sphinxes that are still with us today.

Religion was a part of almost every aspect of the ancient Egyptians' lives. They believed in many gods and goddesses, and they had a deity to help them with just about every problem or threat.

Ancient Egypt was ruled by kings and queens, known as **pharaohs**, who were treated as living gods on earth. The pharaoh performed religious acts called **rituals**. These acts included ceremonies and giving offerings, or gifts, to the gods to ensure that the sun rose every morning, the **Nile River** flooded every summer, and the world continued to exist.

Myths about the gods helped the ancient Egyptians

understand natural occurrences in the world around them. These myths sometimes contradict one another, but to the ancient Egyptians, opposing versions could be true at the same time—this was the magic of the gods. Myths also changed as they were told and retold. Most were shared through oral traditions, meaning they were spoken aloud. There were probably many stories that were never written down and are no longer remembered.

In this book, you're going to discover some of the myths that have been preserved from ancient Egypt. Today, Egyptologists use these stories as a window into a long-extinct culture. Though much has been lost to the sands of time, the magic of these stories, and the incredible artifacts that represent them, continue to inspire us today.

3,500 YEARS OF LIFE ALONG THE NILE

Early Dynastic Period,
circa 3000–2686 BCE

Upper and Lower Egypt become unified, and many familiar aspects of what we think of as ancient Egyptian culture are firmly established.

Old Kingdom,
circa 2686–2160 BCE

King **Djoser** builds the first pyramid at Saqqara, and later kings build the pyramids of Giza and the famous Sphinx.

First Intermediate Period,
circa 2160–2055 BCE

Due to a combination of droughts, the heavy cost of pyramid building, and the loss of the king's power, Egypt becomes divided for about a hundred years, without a central ruler.

Middle Kingdom,
circa 2055–1650 BCE

Egypt is reunited, and this is a time of great literature and intricate art and jewelry.

Second Intermediate Period,
circa 1650–1550 BCE

After a series of weak kings, Egypt falls apart again, with small kingdoms popping up throughout the land.

New Kingdom,
circa 1550–1069 BCE

Egypt is reunited, expands its empire, and reaches its peak in power and wealth. Some of many well-known rulers of this time include pharaohs Hatshepsut, Tut, and Ramesses II.

Third Intermediate Period—Late Period,
1069–332 BCE

Egypt is conquered and controlled by various outside kingdoms, including Libyans, Nubians, Assyrians, and Persians.

Ptolemaic Period,
332–30 BCE

Alexander the Great conquers Egypt and is crowned pharaoh. The Greek Ptolemies rule, including Cleopatra VII, who comes to power as the last pharaoh before the Roman conquest.

Roman Period,
30 BCE–394 CE

Rome rules Egypt, and many Egyptian traditions also continue through the Roman period, including mummification and temple building. With the later spread of Christianity, what we think of as ancient Egyptian culture eventually dies out.

EGYPT, THEN AND TODAY

CITY KEY
Ancient
Modern
Both

Western Desert

Byblos
Syria-Palestine
Sais
Busiris
Bubastis
Nile River
Heliopolis
Cairo
Giza
Memphis
Saqqara
Sinai
Lower Egypt
Eastern Desert
Red Sea
Denderah
Thebes
Luxor
Upper Egypt
Edfu
Nubia
Aswan
Elephantine

RA

(RE, PRE)

The Sun God

Before creation, there was nothing but watery chaos. There existed only the potential for order, the potential for light and dark, and the potential for life. Then something moved, and creation began.

From this chaos, which was called **Nun**, a dark mound rose up. From the center of this mound emerged the creator god, **Atum**, the self-creating one. A **lotus** flower came out of the Nun, holding the sun inside. Together, the sun and Atum created the world. Atum pushed the round, shining orb of the morning sun, and out came Ra, the sun god, who dawned blinding and brilliant.

With this first sunrise, the earth began. Ra created everything on the earth and in the sky: light, darkness, moisture, and ground. Ra brought forth the river, the desert, the air, and the animals out of the Nun. Tears fell down Ra's face, forming the bees that made sweet honey. Ra shaped his children, Shu and Tefnut, from his bodily fluids. In turn, Shu and Tefnut produced their own children: Geb and Nut. Ra ruled all he created, gods and mankind.

Ra rose every morning in the east and began his journey west across the sky on his solar boat. As dusk fell, Ra would sink into the western mountains and continue his travels through the nightly realm below the earth called the **Duat**. There he would face trials and dangers.

Ra had the head of a falcon and the body of a man. A great round **sun disk** sat upon his head. Ra was always the sun, but he would sometimes merge with other gods to create new and powerful forms. These forms often represented the various phases of the sun and its movements. As the infant morning sun, Ra connected with **Khepri**, the beetle form. As the falcon god

Ra-Horakhty, Ra rose up victoriously in the eastern sky. And as the dying sun in the evening, Ra was **Ra-Atum**, and took the form of an old man.

As Ra sank into the western hills, he traveled below the horizon and then entered the underworld. Every night he would change ships from his day boat to his night boat. He rode his night boat with a group of loyal gods. Together, these gods traveled through the caverns of the Duat, facing trials and cavern demons who punished the wicked and threatened the good.

The Duat was made up of the twelve hours of the night. Each nighttime hour related to an underworld goddess who gave Ra new strengths and powers. In turn, Ra gave the goddesses the ability to control the living. At hour six, the middle hour, Ra would meet with the ruler of the underworld, the god Osiris. This meeting made Ra extremely powerful and mighty. More importantly, it allowed Osiris and all the dead people in the underworld to live again.

In hour seven, this new and improved Ra entered the kingdom of his enemy, the huge and powerful snake god **Apophis**. When the two finally met face-to-face, they fought a great battle. Apophis was chaos itself, and Ra's victory against his opponent every night meant his boat could continue back toward the horizon to rise again.

As the sun, Ra had to make this voyage every day and night. If the sun did not rise, move along its daily path through the sky, set, and rise again the next morning, the earth would cease to exist. All life depended on Ra surviving his nightly quest in the underworld.

On earth, the pharaoh was responsible for aiding Ra during his difficult nightly journey. In the **Karnak temple**, Pharaoh enacted rituals to guarantee Ra would triumph. Daily rituals and monthly festivals were celebrated, and the sun was praised as it rose each morning.

At the beginning of the New Kingdom (**circa** 1550 BCE) a new god rose in popularity in Egypt: **Amun**. Like the wind and air, the god Amun was everywhere. Amun's name meant "the hidden one," unseen yet ever present. He was universal. Ra was supreme, but he and Amun merged to form the powerful **Amun-Ra**, a solar deity ruling over all of the earth and sky.

Amun-Ra usually took the form of a man with a long beard and two large feathers atop his head. These feathers represent Amun-Ra's invisible form—wind can be "seen" when it ruffles and moves through feathers.

Pharaohs led armies outside of Egypt to bring back riches and gold in the name of Amun-Ra. Amun-Ra was pleased, and rewarded the king and the people of Egypt with a good flood, abundant crops, and victorious battles.

THE EYE OF RA AND EYE GODDESSES

Wedjat Eye amulet

The **Eye of Ra** was both the god Ra's actual eye and a mythological role enacted by a number of goddesses including Sekhmet, **Mut**, Hathor, Bastet, and Tefnut. The Eye acted on behalf of Ra, but could sometimes also act independently. As a goddess, the Eye of Ra was fiery and vengeful. She could be a sun disk and cobra, but also a lioness, and she used her lion forces to defend her father, Ra, against his enemies.

SHU
AND TEFNUT

(SCHU, CHOU) (TEFENET)

God of Air and Goddess of Moisture

Ra was the creator and ruler of heaven and earth. As a creator god, one of Ra's first acts was to make his children, Shu and Tefnut. Ra sneezed out the god Shu and spat out the goddess Tefnut. Shu was the air and sunlight, dry and flowing. Tefnut was the goddess of holy moisture and morning dew.

Shu's name probably means "he who rises up." This is because Shu separated the earth from the sky. The meaning of Tefnut's name is uncertain, but it might actually refer to the sound you make when you spit! Although they were created as liquids, they often appeared as lion deities.

Ra formed Shu and Tefnut in the city of **Heliopolis**, one of the places in Egypt where the world began. The two children lived with their father and were close to him, hardly leaving his side. One day when they were still young, Shu and Tefnut grew tired of their sheltered life. "Let's travel and discover all that is out there in Nun!" they exclaimed. And so they left the comfort of their father's home, seeking adventure.

Nun is endless, and so Shu and Tefnut never really had to stop exploring. There was always something new to discover. But the endlessness of Nun also meant that the pair could easily lose their way.

Shu and Tefnut were gone for a very long time. Over time Ra grew lonely without them. He wondered where they were and when they might return. "What if they are lost?" he worried.

Ra sent out his powerful eye, the Eye of Ra, to find his children and bring them back to him. The Eye of Ra looked all over the universe. She searched for a very long time. She finally found Shu and Tefnut, but they had been gone for so long that they had become full-grown! They missed their father, too.

The Eye of Ra helped Shu and Tefnut find their way home to Ra, where they were at last reunited. Ra was so happy he cried tears of joy! And these tears turned into humanity—Ra's children on earth.

Having explored the vastness of Nun, Shu and Tefnut were now content to stay near their father and help him however they were able. Tefnut would sometimes wear a headdress that had a sun disk and two cobras. These cobras could spit fire that would protect Ra. Sometimes called "Lady of the Flames," Tefnut was a terrifying lioness who chased off Ra's enemies.

Shu would help bring the sun—his father, Ra—out of the distant mountains each day to make the dawn. Shu was the kingly successor to Ra. After Ra was done being king, Shu took over and ruled the earth, some say for 700 years! Shu would wear great ostrich feathers in his crown that stuck straight up, and he was so large that his walking stride filled the length of the sky.

What happened to end Shu's reign as king is mysterious and uncertain, but it is possible that Shu's wife, Tefnut, and his own son, Geb, overthrew him. However, even when Shu no longer ruled as king, he was praised on earth as the air, and the one who separated the earth from the sky and allowed life to flourish.

ATEN

Relief showing the king, queen, and princesses worshiping the Aten

During his reign, the pharaoh **Akhenaten** and his queen, **Nefertiti**, closed all the temples in Egypt and forbade the worshipping of all gods except the **Aten**, a form of the sun god Ra. The Aten was represented by a sun disk. Some call this the first instance of **monotheism**: the worship of one god. But it didn't last long: after Akhenaten's and Nefertiti's deaths, Egyptians soon went back to worshipping all the gods.

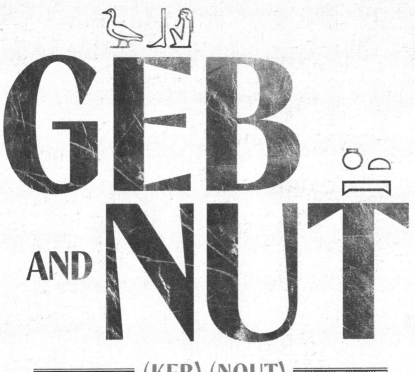

GEB AND NUT

(KEB) (NOUT)

God of the Earth and Goddess of the Sky

G eb and Nut were the children of Shu and Tefnut. This god and goddess were very close and spent all their time together. Geb was the earth and Nut was the sky, but unlike the world today, there was no space between them, meaning the earth and sky touched.

Geb was a man, sometimes with green skin and sometimes with a duck upon his head. He was the land and the dirt below the heavens. Nut could be a woman with a sun disk or a cow speckled with stars. Sometimes she had feathered wings, which she would hold out on either side of her body.

Her body also formed the Duat, or underworld, that existed below the earth. Each morning, Ra would come out of Nut to travel across the daytime sky. Her blood made the morning sky red. Over the course of the day, Ra went through many changes. As evening fell, Ra would be swallowed by Nut as he descended into the Duat again. Meanwhile, the stars traveled through Nut's body during the daylight hours.

Geb ruled as the first king of the earth with Nut at his side. They were deeply in love, but there was no room for anything else to exist between them, including their own children.

Their father, Shu, decided he must do something about the lack of space between Geb and Nut. How could animals live and plants grow when there was no room between the earth and the sky? How could humankind exist?

So Shu squeezed himself between Geb and Nut. He put his feet upon Geb and pushed up on Nut's stomach, separating his two children. Nut went upward and her body formed the sky. She became the stars and heavens. She balanced on her hands and feet, arched over Geb's body, which formed the earth below. Shu held his arms up in the shape of the hieroglyphic sign for the **ka**, or life force. His position reinforced how his act of strength allowed for life on earth to exist.

After some time passed, Shu grew very tired of holding up the sky. He needed help. He created eight **Heh** gods to help him carry the weight of the sky. The Heh gods stood on either side of Shu, and together they all held up Nut.

Geb and Nut's separation is sometimes told as a much later event in the creation story. In this tale, Ra had grown old and become lazy, so humanity rebelled against him. Their plotting against their creator greatly angered Ra, and he punished humanity, but in the end spared them from complete destruction. Ra was exhausted and knew it was his time to leave earth. His daughter Nut changed into a cow and Ra climbed upon her back. Nut pushed Ra, who was a great sun disk, up to the heavens. Nut shook under the heavy weight of the great god, and the Heh gods were created to help her hold up her father.

After Geb and Nut were separated, there was room for life! With Nut's body as the heavens arched above the earth, there was space for Geb and Nut to have children of their own. But one story tells that Ra feared if Nut had children, one of them might one day overthrow him. So he placed a curse upon Nut. Ra said Nut could not give birth on any of the 360 days of the Egyptian year. The crafty god Thoth thought of a way to help her. He won a board game against Aah, a moon god. The winning prize was five extra days of sunlight, and these five days were added to the year and were the days on which Nut's children were born.

Nut gave birth to the gods Osiris, Isis, Seth, and Nephthys. Holidays were celebrated for each of these gods, and for Horus (the son of Isis and Osiris), on the days of their birth—the last five days of the year. These gods were known as the Great **Ennead** of Heliopolis. The divine children of Geb and Nut in turn gave birth to all of humankind.

Even now that they were separated, Geb and Nut did everything together. Geb was the land Egyptians walked upon. Nut created the rain with her tears. When Geb laughed, the earth shook as earthquakes. When Nut laughed, the thunder rolled.

With room for animals and plants to grow, Geb became the keeper of snakes, creatures who burrowed and lived beneath and within the earth. Barley and wheat grew from Geb's ribs, and plants sprouted from his back. He was the source of groundwater, and nourished the earth as both rich soil and life-giving water. Cattle's hooves danced upon his back and ate from his grain ribs, while **Hapy**, a Nile god, was his close friend.

As the ground, Geb also swallowed up the dead and could sometimes represent graves for Egyptians who had passed on. Nut was also a protector of the dead. Her body covered the deceased, and they would become stars in her body. Her picture is often painted along the inside of coffin lids or across the front of the mummy case. She was on tomb walls and ceilings as well. She was present in underworld gardens as the sycamore-fig-tree goddess, providing the deceased with cool water and food on their journey in the afterlife.

Depending on the story, Geb was either Shu's chosen heir or he stole the throne from Shu. Either way, Geb was closely tied to kingship. The pharaohs called themselves "son of Geb." When they died, Nut carried them up to the heavens where they would become one of the undying stars. Some think Nut also represented the Milky Way.

GEOGRAPHY OF EGYPT

The Egyptians' world was made up of the Nile River, the black and green fertile land next to the water where plants grew, and the red desert. Desert, mountains, and sea surrounded Egypt, and this kept it generally isolated from neighboring cultures and invaders . . . but not completely.

NEITH

(NEUTH, NERET)

Goddess of Creation and War

As we have seen, the Egyptians told different stories explaining how the world began. In another version of creation, Nun again existed as nothingness. But this time, within Nun the goddess Neith stirred. Neith turned herself into a fish—then she turned herself into a cow. As the first living being, Neith took on many forms. As her first act, Neith created Egypt. She made the land out of joy. She separated the night from the day.

Neith was worshipped in the earliest days of Egypt, when Upper and Lower Egypt were united by

King Narmer. In those early days, the **symbol** for Neith—an oval with two legs on the top and two on the bottom—was thought by some to be a click beetle. But in later times, this shape was thought to be two arrows crossed over a shield. Neith would often wear this upon her head. Sometimes she wore the **Red Crown** of Lower Egypt instead. As the lady of arrows, she would hold a bow and arrows in her hand.

With seven magic words Neith created the world. She spoke the names of 30 gods and they came into being. Neith told the gods to pull themselves out of the endless and watery Nun and onto the earth.

The gods listened and followed, but they were also worried about who Neith would make next. Neith decided on an all-powerful god, ruler of all: Ra. He would blink, and night would come. He would open his eyes, and day would come. Ra would form other gods from his spit.

The gods were jealous, but there was nothing to be done—their mother ruled.

Neith promised she would protect Ra and strengthen him. She also predicted that his children, mankind, would one day rebel against him. Mankind would not win, however, because Ra would always have the power of his mother, Neith, behind him. Ra would always be king of Egypt. He would be called Khepri the beetle in the morning and Atum the old man in the evening.

Neith formed Ra in an egg. When the egg cracked and he was born, Neith called out to her child, "Come to me!" Ra opened his eyes, and daylight came out and the sun shone for the first time. He could not find his mother, though, and he began crying. From his tears, mankind was created.

Neith knew good could not exist without evil. There must be balance in the universe. And so Neith created Ra's enemy, the great snake Apophis, out of her spit. Apophis was huge, dangerous, and powerful.

When Ra was still young, Apophis gathered his like-minded human friends and they plotted revenge against the sun god. Ra heard about the plan and was angry. The wise god Thoth came out of Ra's heart, and Thoth and Ra talked about what to do about Apophis and his troublesome humans.

Thoth, as the god of learning and words, was very smart. In the end, Thoth set out to meet with Apophis while Ra planned a daring escape from his enemies with his mother, Neith. Neith changed into her cow form, and Ra sat on her head. Neith carried Ra between her cow horns across the Nile River, swimming away from the chaos snake Apophis.

Because of this escape route, Neith was closely associated with water. She sometimes appeared as a large Nile fish called a *Lates*. In connection with water, Neith was also the mother of Sobek, the great crocodile god. She protected water and underground creatures like crocodiles and snakes.

Neith and Ra made it safely to the city of Sais in the north. There Neith took care of her son and helped him grow big and strong. When he was ready, Ra fought and beat Apophis and his other enemies.

Ra grew up to rule the world and lead the sun on its daily journey. And because Neith was Ra's mother, she would sometimes join him on his nightly trips into the underworld. As a hunter and warrior, Neith's arrows were deadly, and as the first mother she protected all: human, crocodile, and Ra. Neith was the great mother, but her name probably meant "the terrifying one." This powerful, ancient goddess was capable of both violence and motherly affection.

Ruins of the Temple of Horus at Edfu

TEMPLES

Temples were the homes of the gods. Their shapes and decoration varied over time and place, but each one included a statue of its god. The king, priests, and priestesses worked in temples, performing rituals for the god. Priests would wash, dress, and leave food for the gods every day. During festivals, the god's statue was carried outside and paraded around the city or sailed down the Nile so everyone had a chance to see the god.

OSIRIS

(USIR)

God of the Underworld

The son of Geb and Nut, Osiris was born when Egypt was still young, divided, and at war. Mankind was uncivilized and Upper and Lower Egypt were not yet united. Osiris was born wearing a crown because he was specially chosen by the sun god, Ra, to eventually follow in the footsteps of his father, Geb, the king.

Osiris first ruled from the town of Busiris in the **Delta**, the marshy area in northern Egypt where the Nile spreads out in multiple directions before dumping into the Mediterranean Sea. But over time Osiris expanded his kingdom across all of Egypt, ruling like his father, Geb, had.

Osiris was a true and just king of Egypt. He ruled Egypt with his beloved sister, Isis. He taught his people how to cultivate the fields, to grow wheat, barley, and vegetables. He instructed mankind about laws and how to live as refined people.

But not everyone loved Osiris. His brother, Seth, was jealous of Osiris and his power. Seth wished to rule himself, and so he set his sights on the throne of Egypt.

Egypt prospered under Osiris. Because things were running smoothly, Osiris decided to leave Egypt and travel east to spread his knowledge and teach others his skills. Seth saw this absence as the perfect opportunity. While Osiris was traveling, Seth began to plot his takeover.

Seth collected 72 coconspirators to enact his plan. "Help me overthrow my brother," he said to them. When Osiris returned to Egypt, Seth and his coconspirators invited him to a great feast. At the party, everyone took their turn lying in a coffin to see if they might fit inside. For some it was too big; for others it was too small. Like Cinderella's slipper, it only fit Osiris's body.

While Osiris was lying in the coffin, Seth and his helpers nailed shut its wooden lid. Osiris was trapped! The conspirators poured piping-hot molten metal into the cracks to fill in the air holes. Osiris could not breathe. Seth had murdered his brother!

Osiris's coffin was thrown into the river and swept downstream by the Nile's currents until it was deposited into the sea. It floated northward and landed at the port of **Byblos**, on the shores of modern-day Lebanon. The coffin came to rest near a tamarack tree. Sensing the god's presence, the tree grew tall and beautiful and covered the wooden case with the dead king inside.

The tree grew so grand that the king of Byblos took notice and cut it down to use in building his palace. The wood, with Osiris inside of it, was used to construct a large pillar. There Osiris remained, his location unknown to all but the tree branches around him.

In death, Osiris became king of the afterlife. Now Osiris dressed in all white, representing the linen wrappings of a mummy, with a **mummiform** body as well. Upon Osiris's head was the **Atef crown**. He held the **crook and flail**, symbols of kingship. Osiris's dark-green skin represented the rich, fertile land next to the Nile where the crops grew best, and it also represented his own rebirth in the afterlife.

The souls of ancient Egyptians traveled to the west when they died, and dead Egyptians were called Westerners. Osiris was "Foremost of the Westerners," or the lord of the dead. As king of the underworld, Osiris ruled and allowed the human dead to be reborn like him.

Still on earth, Isis had no idea where her husband was. She sensed something terrible had happened to him. She fled north to the Delta with her son Horus the Child. As the son of Osiris, Horus could one day have a claim to his father's throne, so he was in danger from Seth. Isis left Horus in the care of the cobra goddess **Wadjet**, who hid the young boy to protect him. Wadjet placed Horus on the island of Khimmes, far away from his uncle.

Isis went looking for her husband up and down the Nile. She feared the worst: that her beloved husband had died. Everywhere she went, Isis asked children if they had seen a coffin.

Eventually she reached Byblos. At the Nahr al-Kalb, the River of the Dog, she met ladies from the court of the Queen of Byblos bathing and doing the washing. Isis washed with them and adjusted their royal jewels, and the women could smell her holy, sweet smell—the smell of a goddess. The smell traveled back with the women to the palace, while sad Isis stayed on the shore. The queen asked where the wonderful smell came from, and when she heard that there was a goddess nearby, she asked that Isis be brought to the palace at once. Isis followed, hoping that in the palace she would finally find a clue to her husband's disappearance.

SHABTIS

Small wood, stone, or ceramic statues often in the shape of mummies, shabtis were placed in tombs to do work for the dead. Shabtis could be inscribed with spells that would bring them to life when they were called, to help with work in the fields and provide food for the deceased forever.

ISIS

(ASET, ESET)

Goddess of Magic, Thrones, and Healing

When Isis arrived at the palace of Byblos, the queen begged for the great goddess's help. The young prince of Byblos was very ill, and the queen pleaded with Isis to save him. As a powerful healer, Isis agreed, but she also had her own motives—once she stepped inside the palace of Byblos, she realized that her husband's body was trapped within the large wooden pillar there!

Isis devoted herself to healing the young prince of Byblos, in the room with the pillar that held Osiris's body inside. Day by day the prince slowly got better, but Isis wouldn't let anyone else watch her work.

The Queen of Byblos grew curious about what Isis was doing to her child. She snuck into the room with the great wooden pillar and hid. She watched as Isis made a huge fire and placed the boy in a space between the burning logs. Isis then changed herself into a sparrow. She flew around the room and around the pillar, crying over Osiris.

The queen was horrified and raced from her hiding spot to save her son from the fire. She sprinted with him down the hall and away from Isis, but the goddess turned into her true form, powerful and huge, and stopped the queen.

"Queen! Why did you do this? The human parts of your son had almost been burned away, and he would have been forever young and alive."

The queen was ashamed. By doubting the goddess, she had cost her son his eternal life.

"Now," Isis went on, "give me the wooden pillar, for it contains the remains of my husband, the great god Osiris."

Surprised and awestruck, the queen and king sent for men to come and break open the pillar. Inside they found the hidden chest with Osiris!

Isis retrieved the chest, and with it the body of her husband. She headed back to Egypt in a **papyrus** boat, and sailed to the island of Khimmes, where she had left her son Horus.

When Isis's boat reached the island, she heard a terrible cry. Her young son had been stung by a scorpion! Leaping from the boat, she ran to him and used her magic healing powers to cure her son's bite. But in her hurry, she had left Osiris's coffin behind in the boat, tucked in the marshes of the Delta.

Seth was hunting in the reeds when he came upon the coffin. Recognizing the box, he broke it open. He tore Osiris's body into many pieces and angrily scattered the parts all over Egypt. He laughed, declaring that he had done the impossible: "I have destroyed the body of a god!"

Isis returned to find the chest broken and her

husband's body ravaged. She knew that jealous Seth was responsible. She climbed into the papyrus boat and sailed around the marshes and Nile, collecting the broken pieces of her husband. To confuse Seth, Isis built shrines—holy buildings—wherever she found a body part, but instead of leaving the parts in the shrines, she kept them with her.

When all the parts were collected, Isis magically restored Osiris to his full form: the first mummy. In his restored state, the green-skinned and powerful Osiris was able to rule as Judge of the Dead in the Duat for eternity.

The ancient Egyptians told more than one version of the famous murder of Osiris. In an earlier story, Seth killed Osiris by knocking him down, trampling him, and drowning him in the Nile. He then chopped Osiris up and spread his body about.

In this version, Isis collected the pieces of Osiris with the help of her sister, Nephthys. They put Osiris back together, magically restoring their king and brother. They became symbols of mourners, loved ones who attend funerals, for living Egyptians.

In other versions of this tale, Horus is not born until after Isis puts Osiris back together. After Horus grows up, Isis works hard and uses all her cunning to help her son take over his father's role as king.

Isis was a wise goddess—maybe the wisest. She knew more than almost anyone, but the one thing even she did not know was the **rn**, the secret and true name of the sun god Ra. So she devised a plan to find out.

One day, in his old age, Ra spat on the earth. Isis took the dirt, wet from his spit, and formed a mud snake. She brought the snake to life and placed it on the path where Ra often walked. Indeed, while Ra was walking a few days later, the snake bit him. The snake's venom caused Ra to shake and tremble, and he did not know what to do.

Ra, thinking he might die, called his family of gods to him to see if any might be able to help him. Isis came, saying, "When a man says his own name, his rn, aloud, a spell can be cast and the venom will leave his body. I will help cure you, Ra, if you tell me your secret name." Ra did not want anyone to know his secret name—but he also did not want to die. He repeated many of his names and his roles as the creator, but none were his true name and so Isis did not heal him.

Finally, Ra gave in on the condition that Isis would only tell her son Horus and no one else. With this secret knowledge, Isis would secure the throne of Egypt for her son Horus. And Isis, as a smart trickster, loyal mother, and powerful healer, kept her end of the bargain and cured Ra, saying, "Ra lives and the venom has died."

MAAT

Maat, Isis, Horus, and Queen Nefertari

The goddess of order and truth, **Maat** was usually depicted as a woman with two large wings or as a single feather. Maat represented order in the universe, while her counterpart, **Isfet**, was disorder. These two aspects needed to be kept balanced. It was the pharaoh's job on earth to make sure Maat was maintained—the Nile kept flowing, the sun kept rising, and the crops kept growing.

HORUS
THE CHILD
AND
HORUS
THE ELDER

(HOR-PA-KHERED, HARPOCRATES)
(HOR, HERU)

Child God of Healing and Falcon God of Kings

Seth wanted to rule Egypt forever, but young Horus—the son of Isis and Osiris—stood in his way. Ra had chosen Horus to be the godly ruler of Egypt, which meant that as long as Horus was around, he was a threat to Seth's authority.

Isis knew that the jealous and ambitious Seth wanted Horus out of the picture. Fearing for her son, Isis hid Horus in the marshes, and the god Atum used his magic to protect the papyrus marshes and keep all other gods out. For years, Horus was safely hidden where Seth could never find him.

Horus the Child wore his hair in a **sidelock** of youth and held his pointer finger to his mouth. This was the typical way Egyptian children looked on tomb walls and in statues. As the son of Isis, Horus could help heal people on earth. Humans prayed to the young god for protection and to feel better.

Meanwhile, his uncle Seth ruled Egypt for many years.

When Horus was full-grown and strong, the young prince left the safety of the magical marshes. He went to the court of gods. No longer Horus the Child, he now had a human body and the head of a falcon. He sat before the group of powerful gods and the lord of all and said, "It is time for me to take my rightful place as king!"

The gods listened, and some supported Horus. But others liked the leader they already had.

Seth said, "I am the strongest! I ride Ra's boat and fight all his enemies like no other god can! The office should be mine!"

The gods debated back and forth: "We should give it to the brother!" "No, we should give it to the son!"

"Let me and Horus go outside and fight in hand-to-hand combat," Seth suggested, knowing he was physically stronger than Horus. "The winner will be king!"

Instead, the gods brought in **Banebdjede**, a ram-headed god, to judge between Horus and Seth. The ram-headed god looked at Horus and Seth, and he did not know what to do either! "Let's send a letter to the great goddess Neith so she can decide," he suggested. "What she says is what we will do."

The gods wrote the letter to Neith, asking whether Horus or Seth should be crowned. She replied quickly, saying, "Give the office of Osiris to his son, Horus. Give Seth great wealth and loyal friends. This is the right thing to do. If not, there will be great trouble."

But Seth did not care what Neith said. He did not want only wealth and friends. He wanted to be the ruler of Egypt, no matter what it took . . .

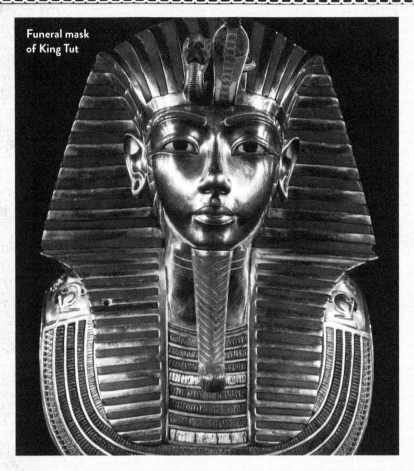

Funeral mask of King Tut

PHARAOH

Pharaoh, meaning "great house," was one of the words for king in ancient Egypt. The king was believed to be a living god. The pharaoh was responsible for making the sun rise each morning and the Nile flood each year. Pharaoh was the living Horus on earth and Osiris, the ruler of the underworld, in death.

SETH

(SET)

God of Deserts, Storms, War, and Chaos

After killing his brother, Osiris, Seth ruled Egypt for at least 100 years. But now that Horus was grown up and ready to claim his crown, Seth was trapped in a long struggle with his nephew to hold on to the office of king.

Seth was an unknown creature called the Seth animal. He had four legs; long, square-topped ears; and a long, thin tail that pointed up to the sky. He was lord of storms and of the desert, the "red land." He was connected to many types of wild beasts. In the form of a donkey, Seth trampled on grain that represented his brother, Osiris. As a hippo, Seth was locked in constant battle with Horus.

Although Seth murdered his brother, Osiris, it was not all bad—Osiris was destined to be king of the underworld. Osiris's death was in some ways meant to be. But Seth's reign as king was not.

The gods brought Seth and Horus to an island where they could judge which of them should become king. They ordered the ferryman, Nemty, not to give Isis a ride to the island, because they knew that if she were there, she would continue to meddle.

Isis did not want to leave her son Horus on an island with Seth and the other gods, where she could not take care of him. Disguised as an old woman, Isis tried to bribe Nemty with cake, but he would not ferry her across. Isis then pulled out a gold ring and for that, he agreed to take her.

When Isis arrived on the island she changed into a beautiful woman—a woman the gods would not recognize. When Seth saw her, he immediately fell in love with the beautiful stranger.

Seth hid behind a sycamore tree and called out to her. Isis said, "Hello, great lord! I come to you to beg for your help. I was the wife of a cattle herder, and he and I had a son. When my husband died, my son watched over the cattle, but one day a stranger came. He said to my son, 'I will beat you, take your father's cattle, and send you away!' I need someone to speak on behalf of my son. Who do you think is in the right here?"

Seth listened and sympathetically responded, "Of course, you and your son are in the right. How could this stranger take your husband's cattle when his son still lives?"

With that, Isis magically changed into a kite, a bird of prey, and flew up into an acacia tree. She yelled down to Seth, "You have just judged against yourself!"

Seth could not believe it! He had been tricked. Ra-Horakhty said to him, "You have just judged a very similar situation to your own in favor of the son. That should tell you what the right answer is."

But Seth did not want to accept it. He challenged Horus to a contest. "Horus, let's change into hippopotamuses and dive deep down into the sea. There, we will wait. Whoever comes up before three months is over loses the office of king!" Horus agreed. They changed into hippos and dived down together.

Isis watched in horror as her son dove. "Once they are in the depths of the sea, with no one to stop him, Seth will kill my son!" she exclaimed. "I must protect him!"

Isis made a copper spear, tied a rope to one end, and threw it into the water. It pierced the hide of a hippopotamus. But it was not Seth. The spear had hit Horus!

Horus cried out, "Ouch!" and Isis quickly used her magic to pull the spear back up.

She threw it again, and this time she hit Seth. Now Seth yelled out in pain. He begged Isis to let him go. "Remember that I am your brother," he cried out to her. And in that moment, Isis was overcome with compassion. She pulled the spear free, releasing Seth.

Horus was furious. He felt that his mother had betrayed him. He jumped out of the water and, with a roar, he cut off her head with a large knife!

But because Isis was a goddess, she could not really die. Instead, she turned herself into a headless stone statue.

Horus knew the gods would punish him for hurting his mother, so he ran away to an **oasis** in the Western Desert. He hid—but not well enough. Seth found him there. Seth grabbed Horus, threw him down, and cut out his eyes.

Seth buried the eyes, and two lotus flowers grew out of them the next morning. He went back to the court and lied to the gods, telling him he had not found his nephew.

Hathor, goddess of love, did not believe Seth, so she went out in search of Horus. She found him blind and crying. Hathor found a wandering gazelle, milked the creature, and poured the milk over Horus's eyes. Horus could see again! Hathor went back to the gods and told them, "I found Horus in an oasis, and he had no eyes thanks to Seth."

Ra-Horakhty sent Seth and Horus away. "Go work this out on your own and leave us in peace!" he said. "We are tired of your fighting."

The two went off to Seth's house, where Seth made a feast for Horus. But Horus should not have trusted his uncle! When Horus was asleep that night, Seth attacked him. Isis came and rescued her son, and the gods were angry with Seth's underhanded tactics.

From the underworld, Osiris spoke up. "If you do not resolve this, I will send my messengers of violence to hunt you all, and they are not scared of any god."

Seth still tried to continue the fight, but the gods heeded Osiris and made their decision. Horus should be king! They had Isis bring Seth in chains, and they placed the **White Crown** upon Horus's head, this time for good. At last, Horus was king.

Although Seth's reign was over, he remained popular with kings and common Egyptians alike for his strength and battle smarts. He was the lord of metals, and carried an impossibly heavy scepter. Seth, he who thunders in the sky, could be a force of chaos and craziness. But Seth was necessary to keep balance in the world of the living and dead.

Great Pyramids at Giza

PYRAMIDS

Many kings and queens of the Old and Middle Kingdoms (circa 2686–1650 BCE) built pyramids for their tombs. These aboveground structures had four triangular sides and a square base. Their sloping sides represented the rays of the sun and Ra. Djoser's Step Pyramid was the first, but the Great Pyramid at Giza was the largest. Many pyramids, or their ruins, still stand to this day.

NEPHTHYS

AND
THE FOUR SONS
OF HORUS

(NEBET HUT)

Goddess of the Dead and Guardians of the Dead

I f you were to die in ancient Egypt, one of the most important things would have been for your body to stay intact so that you could have an afterlife. A team of gods and goddesses, including Nephthys and the Sons of Horus, work together to ensure that what happened to Osiris—the pieces of his body scattered everywhere—will not happen to anyone else. You would be mummified so your body, and thus your soul, could last forever.

During mummification, four important organs are removed from your body: the lungs, liver, stomach, and intestines. These organs are then placed in **canopic jars**, which are laid in the burial chamber along with your mummy. These jars need extra safeguarding. Fortunately, the Sons of Horus are here to help.

The Sons of Horus are four male gods who are each assigned a body part: Hapy the baboon protects the lungs, Imsety the human protects the liver, Duamtef the jackal watches over the stomach, and Qebehsenuef the falcon protects the intestines. They are each connected with a geographic location, too—north, south, east, and west.

Sons of Horus **amulets** are placed on your body and strung and sewn into your mummy wrappings to magically help keep the body parts safe and in place. These four gods' heads are included on the tops of the canopic jars, so that you can easily recognize which body part is where.

The Sons of Horus travel with you on your journey through the underworld. Your mummy as well as the parts of your soul—your heart, or **ib**, your personality, or **ba**, and your life force, or ka—are all in danger during your afterlife trip to paradise. You need all the help you can get!

But the Sons of Horus do not act alone. Each has a female counterpart. Nephthys protects Hapy and the lungs, Isis helps Imsety with the liver, Neith teams up with Duamtef on the stomach, and the scorpion goddess Serqet works with Qebehsenuef to protect the intestines.

Of these four goddesses, Nephthys is the most involved in funerals. She is your close and constant companion in death. She oversees your organs as they are placed within their correct canopic jars. Nephthys is both the youngest and most recognizable of Nut and Geb's children—her striking crown is made of the two **hieroglyphs** for her name, Nebet-Hut, meaning "lady of the mansion."

Nephthys was Seth's wife, but like all the gods and goddesses of Egypt, Nephthys was a complicated figure, and she was not always trustworthy. She loved Osiris, too, and tricked him into having a baby with her. In some stories, this baby grew up to become the god Anubis, the jackal-headed god of the cemetery and the underworld.

After Seth murdered Osiris, Nephthys joined Isis in weeping over the death of their brother, and she helped her sister look for the pieces of Osiris's body. Seth had scattered them throughout the land, but together Nephthys and Isis were able to find them. Isis magically healed Osiris, making him whole again.

After Osiris had been put back together, he needed to be mummified. Anubis, the god of mummification, worked with Isis to mummify Osiris. But they needed Nephthys, too. Nephthys was known for her skills as a weaver, and so she expertly helped wrap Osiris's body in linens. The ancient Egyptians connected Nephthys closely with linen bandages and mummification—they believed that mummy wrappings were made from the tresses of Nephthys's hair. As your body is wrapped during the mummification process, Nephthys's locks, too, surround your every toe, finger, and limb to protect them.

Just as Nephthys protected the body of Osiris, she also helped safeguard the bodies of the human dead. In ancient Egypt, Nephthys and Isis were central to every funeral. Women dressed up like the two goddesses will join your family and friends, crying and wailing over your body, just as the goddesses cried over Osiris.

On coffins, Nephthys was painted at the head, while Isis was painted on the feet. The pictures of the goddesses forever watch over your remains.

Canopic jars

MUMMIFICATION

In order to live after death, Egyptians believed a body needed to be preserved. Priests created mummies by drying out the body for about 70 days with natron (salt) and saying spells. The lungs, stomach, liver, and intestines were removed and placed in canopic jars, while the brain was thrown out. The body was wrapped in linen and covered with amulets.

ANUBIS

(ANPU, INPU)

God of Mummification

With the body of a human and the head of a long-nosed, doglike jackal, Anubis defended the dead. Egyptians prayed to Anubis to protect their dead family members from the teeth of wild dogs that scavenged in graveyards, from the destructive passage of time, and from the dangerous journey through the underworld.

The most important body that Anubis ever protected was Osiris's. After Osiris was murdered, Seth wanted to destroy Osiris's body as it lay in the marshes. Seth changed himself into a leopard so he would not be recognized. Anubis came to the body's defense. He grabbed Seth and branded him with a hot iron, which covered Seth's fur in dark spots where he had been burned. And that's how leopards got their spots.

It was necessary that Anubis protect the body of Osiris, and of every Egyptian so they could have a successful afterlife. A priest wearing an Anubis mask would be the one to mummify your body.

After death and mummification, your family prepares for your burial. Anubis performs the **Opening of the Mouth ceremony**, saying prayers and spells to open your eyes, mouth, and ears so you can use your senses in the afterlife. Now you are ready to be reborn!

Your body is placed in a coffin and laid in your tomb. Hopefully your family and friends will have left you food, drink, spells, and maps to help you make it through the afterlife. You must be ready to make the difficult journey to the **Hall of Judgment**, where you will meet Osiris, king of the Duat—the underworld.

After your burial, Anubis will prowl the top of the desert cliffs overlooking the graveyard, so he can protect your body. But your soul will not remain there. It will join the sun and travel into the western horizon, where you become a Westerner—one of the dead. Your soul now moves below the earth where you are left to face the underworld on your own.

You have entered the afterlife, but before you can live happily forever in the **Field of Reeds**, the place where the blessed dead live, you must prove you have lived a good life on earth. You will meet many difficulties on your path to meet Osiris, including giant hippos and lakes of fire! You use spells to fight and to journey safely, and you call upon the gods to help you.

After passing through many gates and defeating wild beasts, you will at last make it to the Hall of Judgment! It is Anubis's job to greet you. He is proud you have made it this far, and he brings you inside the court.

The court is filled with gods, and Anubis tells them of all the good things you have done in your life. At last, he says, "We shall now weigh your heart against Maat, the feather of truth!" In ancient Egypt, your heart, or ib, is where all your thoughts and actions come from. The heart knows everything you have done.

Osiris oversees the court and the weighing of the heart ceremony. A scale is set up. Your heart is placed on one side, while the feather of Maat is placed by Anubis on the other side. The god Thoth will write down the results.

On one side of the court, **Ammut**, the "devourer" monster, waits. She is a ferocious beast with the head of a crocodile, the mane of a lion, and the body of a hippopotamus. If your heart is heavier than the feather, she will eat it, and you will have no afterlife.

The gods want to be sure that you will be able to survive in the afterlife. While the weighing takes place, you must list all the bad things you have *not* done in your life. Thank goodness your family made a beautiful papyrus scroll for you that has the spells you need written down! "I have not stolen anything. I have not murdered. I have done no harm. I have not cheated when giving gifts to the gods. I have said no lies. I have not eavesdropped or made up false tales about someone. I have not been rude. I have not cursed the king nor the gods."

You have recited everything correctly! Thanks to Anubis's assistance, you have passed all the tests and proven yourself to have lived a good life. On the scale, your heart is balanced with Maat, with truth. You are free to go through the final gate and be received by Osiris, lord of the afterlife.

You will now begin your new life among the living dead. There is a great feast and you are forever blessed, living a good eternal life in the Field of Reeds.

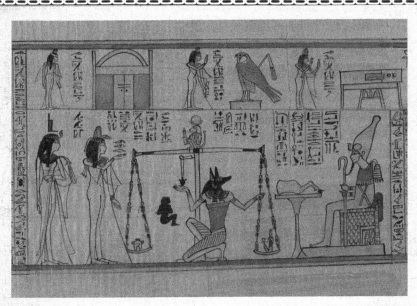

THE AFTERLIFE AND THE SOUL

Anubis weighing the heart against the feather of Maat, from the *Book of the Dead*

Ancient Egyptians believed when people died they would travel to the Duat, or underworld, to the Field of Reeds, or paradise. The body, or het, was mummified so that parts of the soul, called the ka and ba, could live on. The ka was the life force, while the ba was an individual's uniqueness and personality. Statues were built in tombs to give the ka of the dead places to inhabit.

SERQET

(SERKET, SELKIS)

Goddess of Scorpions

Seth had just murdered his brother, Osiris, the king of Egypt, so he himself could become king. Isis, Osiris's wife, knew that Seth would not stop until he had done everything to ensure the office of king was his forever, and that there would never be another god who had a claim to the throne. Isis was pregnant with her son Horus, who was set to be the future king, and so was a threat to Seth's throne. To save herself and her unborn child, Isis needed to hide from her violent brother Seth. And so Isis called upon Serqet, the goddess of scorpions, for protection.

Serqet was the funerary goddess who helped Qebehsenuef protect the canopic jars holding the intestines of the dead. Serqet looked like a human woman, but on her head sat a venomous scorpion, ready to strike. Scorpions and their stings were one of the great threats to the ancient Egyptians, particularly young children and the weak elderly. When **scribes** wrote Serqet's name, they would often leave out the scorpion hieroglyph, or they would draw a harmless water scorpion in its place. Hieroglyphs were magic, and the scribes worried that the image of a venomous scorpion could come to life and attack! Serqet's venom was dangerous, but she used her power to defend the living from stings and bites.

Serqet enacted her scorpion magic to help those who needed her—and to attack those who opposed her. When she rode on Ra's solar ship as he made his journey through the Duat, her venom came in handy! She helped Ra to tie up his enemy, the snake god Apophis, during their great nightly battle. In your journey through the Duat into the afterlife, Serqet guarded a tricky twist in the river, and would help you through that path.

Serqet heard Isis's cry for protection and replied, "Isis, my sister, of course I will help you!" Serqet magically divided herself into seven scorpions, dangerous and fierce guardians. This team of seven surrounded Isis and brought her safely into the marshes, far away and safe from Seth.

With Serqet's help, Isis reached a marsh village and went up to the home of a rich woman. "Please let me in," Isis begged.

The woman took one look at pregnant Isis, who was dirty and tired from her journey, and stuck up her nose. She did not recognize the goddess. "You cannot stay here!" the rich woman exclaimed, turning her back on Isis.

A young, poor woman who lived in the marshes saw what had happened between the rich woman and Isis. She took pity on the stranger, and told Isis she could stay with her in her modest hut.

Serqet, as the seven scorpions, was furious with the rich woman. How could anyone treat Isis this way? She would get revenge on the rich woman for her selfishness. The seven scorpions put all their venom together into the largest of them all. This deadly creature sneakily crawled into the home of the rich woman and stung her baby.

Isis, who was sleeping in the humble hut, woke to the cries of the rich woman down the road. "My poor child! He is stung!"

Isis ran to the rich woman's house to see what was going on. She felt sorry for the baby. His mother's selfishness and judgment were not his fault. So Isis used her magic to draw the venom out of his tiny body.

Serqet's scorpion powers, as Isis knew, could be used to both cause pain and heal. Serqet's full name, Serqet Hetit, means "she who causes the mouth to breathe." A scorpion could take your last breath with its powerful sting, but Serqet could also restore it and help you live again.

Isis knew the secret names of the seven scorpions of Serqet. With this knowledge, Isis was able to help the baby breathe strong once again.

Now that Isis had saved her child, the rich woman recognized her for the goddess she truly was. "Oh, Isis, thank you so much!" she exclaimed. She wanted to repay Isis for her kindness. But what could a mere human give to a goddess who already had everything! Instead, the rich woman gave all her possessions to the poor woman of the marsh who had helped Isis.

THE TWO LADIES

Hieroglyphic relief of Nekhbet and Wadjet at Karnak Temple in Luxor

Egypt was composed of two regions, Upper and Lower Egypt, and each of these regions was watched over by a goddess. Together these goddesses were the "two ladies," **Nekhbet** and **Wadjet**. Nekhbet was a vulture who guarded Upper Egypt, while Wadjet watched over Lower Egypt as a cobra. Together they protected the united Egypt.

HATHOR

(HUT HERU)

Goddess of Love, Music, and Celebration

It was a lovely day, and Hathor was preparing for an important journey. She put on her finest dress, applied the sweetest perfumes, and did her makeup. The goddess of love, dancing, music, and parties, Hathor was a beautiful woman in her long, dark wig, wearing a sun disk crown between her two cow horns.

Hathor boarded a boat and sailed north on the Nile. She was traveling from her home in Denderah to meet

Horus, the falcon-headed god of Edfu. The two were set to marry. The wedding would not be happening in Horus's temple, but in a small temple along the Nile a little to the north.

Horus's heart jumped when he saw his beautiful Hathor. Their wedding was a very merry event, the celebrations lasting for 14 days.

The people sang of the wonders of Hathor: She was beautiful, her face shone, she was sweet, and she was musical. They sang of the goddess's power—she could control the Nile, tell the flood to come, command the wind. She brought new animals and plants and all good things with her.

Hathor also ruled in the sky. She would become a cow and her body would be the heavens. Her name, Hathor, meant "house of Horus." It referred to the sky, the place where Horus lived when he was a flying falcon. Hathor would sometimes help her father, Ra, move across the sky, picking up the sun with her head as it rested between her horns.

The ancient Egyptians saw cows as protective mothers, for they nursed and cared for their young.

Many goddesses took on cow forms when they acted as mothers. As a cow, Hathor was the mother of many young gods.

Hathor was so maternal that there are some stories in which she was not Horus's wife, but instead acted as a motherly figure to him. In these versions, she watched over and nurtured Horus when he was a baby, hiding in the marshes from his uncle Seth. In her cow form, Hathor breastfed the young king Horus. The pharaoh was Horus on earth, and so Hathor was sometimes shown nursing the young living king, giving him godly power and strength through her magical cow's milk.

While she gave life and power to the living as a mother, Hathor also helped the dead as Mistress of the West. She watched over the dead in their difficult transition from death to new life. She helped when the living went to the tombs to visit their ancestors. Great festivals were celebrated among the tombs, with feasts and songs to Hathor.

Hathor also could take the form of the Seven Hathors. In this role, she welcomed the dead to the afterlife. The dead could drink the milk of these seven cows and live off Hathor's powers in the afterlife. These cows could also tie up demons and bad creatures with their red ribbons.

Hathor cared for everyone in both life and in death. She was a loving parent to all who needed one. She protected the Egyptians who traveled to Byblos for cedarwood and to the Sinai for blue turquoise, and she protected the expeditions that went south to the land of Punt to fetch sweet-smelling incense and precious materials to bring back to Egypt.

But like any parent, even Hathor could sometimes run out of patience. When Hathor became angry, she developed an entirely different identity. When that happened, she even had a new name: Sekhmet.

MUSIC IN ANCIENT EGYPT

We do not know what Egyptian music sounded like, but we know they played rattles (**sistrum** and beaded menits), drums, harps, flutes, and a variety of other instruments. Female musicians often held high status in society, particularly compared to male musicians. Songs were often performed to praise the deities, especially Hathor.

Sistrum

SEKHMET

(SAKHMET)

Goddess of Power, War, and Plague

Hathor was the goddess of love, music, and celebration. But she had a dark side, too. Sometimes she became a dangerous lioness with the body of a woman, a feline head, and a sun disk crown. In this form she was called Sekhmet. As Sekhmet, she had the power to destroy humanity.

Harsh illnesses were thought to be messengers of Sekhmet. When the seasons changed, disease was an especially present danger. During these transitions,

Sekhmet was given extra attention. Rituals, spells, and festivals were held to ask the goddess to spare the people from sickness and to heal those who suffered from the plagues she brought.

Sekhmet was a fierce warrior, so pharaohs often brought her into battle with them. Her arrows were powerful, and they spat illness and disease at the enemies of Egypt. However, the seven arrows of Sekhmet could be a threat against ancient Egyptians, too, so spells were said to protect against them.

One day, though, these spells were not enough to hold back Sekhmet. It happened that Ra had grown old, and the people on earth were no longer showing him respect. They left no food and drink offerings, and no precious jewels and metals in the temples.

This neglectful behavior greatly angered Ra. He had created humankind, but now they were acting as if they did not need him. The best solution, Ra decided, was to destroy mankind and start creation anew. But before he destroyed mankind, Ra spoke with the eldest of all gods, Nun. "Oh great and ancient god, humanity is conspiring against me, but I will not slay them until I have your word." Nun responded, "Behold, Ra, summon Hathor to act as your Eye and slaughter these evil plotters!" And so Ra called upon his daughter Hathor to take the form of the violent Eye goddess Sekhmet and to use her lioness powers to enact his revenge and wipe out the thankless people on earth.

Humanity fled to the wilds of the desert, but strong and fierce Sekhmet hunted them down. They stood no chance. She chased them through the deserts and valleys where they were hiding. None were safe from Sekhmet. She showed no mercy. "The destruction of mankind is an ointment to my heart," she cried to her father.

Ra knew that he had regained power over humanity, but as he watched, he grew sorry for the humans. He had created them and had once loved them. He regretted sending his daughter to kill them all. He asked Sekhmet to stop the violence, but now she had a taste for blood and she wanted more. She could not stop. Soon, humankind would cease to exist.

Ra knew how much Sekhmet loved beer. He ordered 7,000 jars of beer to be brewed. The other gods brought Ra a huge amount of red ochre dye and they mixed it into the beer. While she slept, Ra poured the liquid over the fields where Sekhmet planned to hunt the next day.

When the lioness awoke the next morning she saw the fields soaked in what looked like fresh blood. She lapped it up like sweet milk. The goddess drank until her stomach could hold no more. The huge amount of beer distracted Sekhmet. She fell asleep, purring like a kitten, and thus mankind was saved.

Great Sphinx at Giza

SPHINX

A sphinx was a creature with the body of a lion and the head of a human. The most famous is the Great Sphinx at Giza, a huge stone statue built by the Old Kingdom pharaoh Khafre. The Great Sphinx guarded the pyramids of Khafre and Giza and the large surrounding cemeteries.

BASTET

(BAST, BOUBASTIS, PASHT)

Goddess of Cats, Joy, and Motherhood

B astet was a symbol of motherhood. She was a protector of the home and of pregnant mothers and children. Originally, she had the head of a lioness and the body of woman. But over time, she took the form of a gentler cat. She could be as fickle as a feline—loving and sweet, but also dangerous and destructive. She was closely associated with housecats, and ancient Egyptians often wore cat amulets in both life and death for magical protection.

One day, Bastet's temper rose so furiously that the angry goddess stormed off to the desert. She wandered the wilds and the southern land of **Nubia**, hunting at will and causing mischief. She was gone for so long that her father, the sun god Ra, began to miss her, and he longed for her return.

As the sun set each evening, Ra rode his sun ship through the dangerous Duat, the underworld. Bastet often rode at the bow of his ship, protecting him. Ra's greatest enemy was the snake god Apophis, and nightly they engaged in battle, with Bastet defending her father. Completing this journey meant that the sun was able to rise again the next morning. Bastet helped keep order in the world by ensuring the survival and victory of Ra each night. With Bastet out in the wilderness, Ra was in danger.

The arrival of the yearly Nile flood was critical for the Egyptians. Each summer it brought the water that filled the fields to allow farming and new life. In Bastet's absence the flood had ceased. Egypt grew dry and the crops did not grow. Everyone needed her to come home.

Ra asked the god Shu and the wise god Thoth to convince Bastet to stop her hunting and return to Egypt peacefully. Disguised as baboons, the two gods journeyed south to find her. They tried to convince Bastet to return to Egypt, but she refused. She was happy in the desert. Thoth praised her and spoke of how Egypt was in trouble without her, how its people yearned for her, and how Egypt needed only her to set things right again.

Eventually Bastet gave in to Thoth's compliments. While they traveled north, Thoth amused her with stories, while many Nubian musicians and entertainers joined the group. They soon reached Egypt, much to the happiness of its citizens. The goddess traveled from town to town, delivering water for the plants and bringing the Nile's yearly flood with her from the south. When she reached her father, Ra, he was overjoyed. Egypt was green and filled with crops again.

Bastet's role as an Eye of Ra goddess and the deliverer of the flood was celebrated through festivals and celebrations in the streets and at her main temple in

Bubastis, a city in the north in the eastern Delta of Egypt. This was ancient Egypt's New Year's Day.

Herodotus, known as the father of history, was a Greek man who lived around 450 BCE. He journeyed all across the ancient world, including Egypt, recording his experiences and observations. His firsthand account is an important source for us today. When in Egypt, he visited the monuments (the pyramids were already 2,000 years old!) and spoke with priests and everyday Egyptians.

Herodotus witnessed the Festival of Bastet, and described it as a huge celebration with dancing and feasting and an "anything goes" mentality—similar to Mardi Gras today. According to him, it was the largest and most carefree of the religious festivals. The people celebrated by overeating and drinking, playing music and singing. Sistrum, an instrument similar to a rattle, and menits, short paddles with strings of beads tied to one end, were shaken by priests and priestesses to welcome home the goddess and greet the arrival of the yearly flood in all its richness.

CATS IN ANCIENT EGYPT

Container for a cat mummy

Because the ancient Egyptians thought of Bastet as a cat, they also loved all living cats. Cats were praised as protective and powerful deities, as well as kept as beloved pets, sometimes shown at their owner's feet. The ancient Egyptians even mummified cats and buried them in cat cemeteries at Bastet's temple at Bubastis. There, hundreds of cats were offered to the goddess to ask her for favors in return.

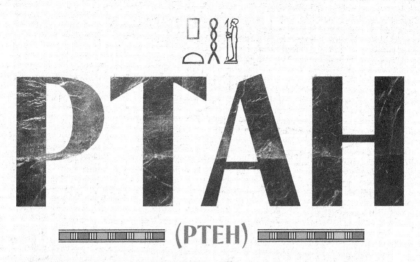

PTAH
(PTEH)
God of Craftsmen

In the beginning, some said, the great god Ptah existed alone. He was supreme, the most powerful god. From inside the mound of creation, Ptah's heart thought and Ptah's tongue spoke, and the gods were born from him.

Ptah was so powerful that his heart and tongue continued to exist within all the deities he created. He was part of everything he made. Ptah lived within every human man and woman, in all cattle, and in every crawling animal. Ptah controlled all actions and movements, all work and crafts, all words and thoughts.

Ptah acted through Shu, and pushed up the sky away from the ground as if it were as light as a feather. He acted through Horus and united the two lands, Upper and Lower, creating one Egypt.

Ptah created laws and morals for Egypt. He said, "Good things will be done to those who behave, and punishment will be done to those who misbehave. The peaceful are given life, the troublemakers are given death!"

Ptah looked at all he had created, and he was pleased. He had formed and given birth to the gods, and he had made the towns and districts of Egypt. He placed the gods and goddesses in their shrines and religious buildings and set up their statues. He gave them each offerings of food and drink. The gods were able to go inside their statues, which were made of wood, stone, clay, or metal. Inside the statues they could enjoy their gifts. These offerings allowed the gods to live and grow on earth.

Ptah was a mummiform human figure. He stood straight with his arms bent, hands holding an **ankh** scepter in front of him. He wore three rows of broad collars tied behind his neck. On his head he wore a tight skullcap. Sometimes a cobra would sit on his forehead.

Ptah lived in the capital city of Egypt, **Memphis**, with the goddess Sekhmet and their son, **Nefertum**. Ptah was a great craftsman and builder. He was kind to his people and his gods. The living Egyptians loved him, and the dead depended upon him. As a craftsman, Ptah would construct new bodies for the dead. Ptah also helped these bodies come back to life in the underworld.

But these bodies could not enjoy the afterlife, as their senses had been left behind. What good was eternal paradise without sight, sound, or taste? So Ptah invented the Opening of the Mouth ceremony. The Opening of the Mouth brought the senses back to life—the eyes and mouth were opened, and the ears could hear once more. The humans were grateful and praised Ptah. Priests performed this important ritual on mummies and on ka statues so that the dead could come to life to eat and drink the treats their family members left in their tombs.

There came a time when King Djoser, a powerful king

of Egypt, began to worry about what would happen when he passed on. He wanted to be remembered by building the most lasting and fantastic tomb, and so he called upon **Imhotep**. Imhotep was an architect and a magical priest, a god of learning and medicine. He was also the son of the great Ptah. Imhotep built the Step Pyramid at Saqqara for his king—the first pyramid! He was praised throughout Egyptian history for his learning and healing powers.

At Saqqara near the Step Pyramid were the tomb and temple of the great **Apis Bull**, a bull who had been identified as the living ba and earthly messenger of Ptah. He was an **oracle** and could foretell what was to be.

When the current Apis Bull died, his death brought sadness throughout the land. A search for a new calf began. The high priests of Ptah traveled up and down the Nile until they found a young calf with the correct markings—it was Ptah reborn!

The calf and its mother were brought to Memphis. On the full moon, the priests crowned the calf as the new Apis Bull. Everything the bull did was watched and recorded because his actions could predict the future. But of course, his power and knowledge came from Ptah, because he was Ptah on earth.

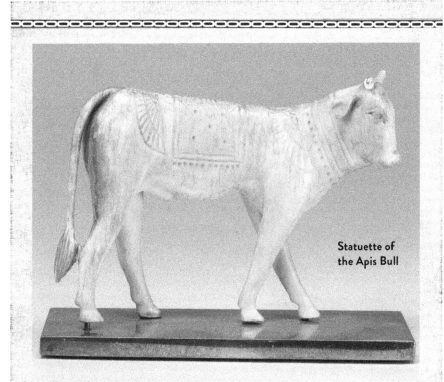

Statuette of
the Apis Bull

ORACLES

When an ancient Egyptian had an important question in their life, they could visit the temple of a god or goddess who was an oracle. Often to answer the question, there would be a written response, or a statue of the god would be moved toward a specific person.

THOTH

(DJEHUTI, TEHUTI)

God of Knowledge, Writing, and Scribes

After creation, there was a time when the world was without words. People had almost no way to communicate with one another, or to remember their deeds or the accomplishments of their ancestors. They would have cried out for help, but they had no words to speak. Thoth, the moon god, changed all of this.

The birth of Thoth is uncertain. He was a god without a mother, and there were many stories about his creation. Thoth may have come from the lips of Ra or he may have even jumped out of Ra's forehead! Some said the great god Ra saw that the world needed order and needed words and communication. Ra made Thoth to keep Maat—the Egyptian concept of order and justice—in the world.

Another tale says Thoth actually created himself. After his self-creation, Thoth took the form of an ibis bird and laid a mythical egg. Inside this egg was all of creation, and all the knowledge of the world.

Once he was born, Thoth saw the distress of the humans, with no way to speak to one another. Through his knowledge and magic, Thoth created hieroglyphs and all the languages. The Egyptians called hieroglyphic writing "the gods' speech." Thoth taught the gods and some select humans how to read and write, and how to have access to knowledge. Thoth also introduced law, art, medicine, literature, and building to the world. Without Thoth, so much of Egyptian culture would have never existed!

Thoth was closely connected with the moon, and as the moon, Thoth had a close relationship with the sun god, Ra. When Ra made his nighttime journey through the Duat, Thoth came to oversee the significant meeting between Ra and Osiris, the ruler of the underworld. Thoth wrote everything down in Ra's absence, and every morning he would tell Ra all that had happened on earth. Ra sent Thoth to other gods as his main messenger. Thoth was fair and worked hard to keep peace between the gods. But he was also clever, and could convince gods and humans of many things.

Once, for example, when angry Bastet ran off to the deserts of Nubia, Thoth, as an intelligent and persuasive messenger, followed her. Disguised as a baboon or an ibis, Thoth finally convinced the goddess to return to Egypt. Her return brought joy and the flood, which Egypt's health depended upon.

Because Thoth sometimes took the form of a baboon, every morning, when the sun rose, baboons across Egypt yelled and screeched and raised their hands to the sky, celebrating Thoth. Other times he chose to appear as an ibis, a long-beaked bird. His thin beak looked like a crescent moon, and the black and white feathers of the ibis bird were like the moon as it grew and shrank in shape over the course of a month. Whenever Egyptian kings died, Thoth carried them between his ibis wings up to the heavens, where they existed as stars for all eternity.

In all of his forms, Thoth could be shown holding a decorated eye. This was called a **wedjat eye**. With its black outline and markings, it represented a falcon's eye, and it symbolized goodness and wholeness. The wedjat eye was an important symbol for the Egyptians, and it appeared in many pictures and amulets.

Thoth was the head **scribe**, or professional writer, and was the wisest of the gods. All human scribes were his close followers and worshippers. Aside from the king and some important priests and administrators, few people had access to Thoth's knowledge. This was because hieroglyphs and religious information were kept a secret from many.

Thoth wrote an epic work called the *Book of Thoth*, a text that contained all the knowledge in the world. It was made up of 42 volumes, the contents of which were mysterious. Only those who promised to use the book's knowledge well and justly were allowed to read it.

The *Book of Thoth* showed how dangerous knowledge and magic could be. One day, a prince named Naneferkaptah greatly desired to have the *Book of Thoth* for himself. When walking through the temple of Ptah one day, an old priest laughed at him.

"You are reading unimportant things. There is a book by Thoth that contains two spells. When you recite the first, you will know the speech of the birds and the beasts of the world and underworld. When you say the second spell, you will be able to see Ra and all his gods."

Naneferkaptah responded, saying, "Tell me where this book is!" He paid the priest for the book's location and set off to retrieve the book, which was hidden in an iron box in the Nile near the town of Coptos.

The book was guarded by Thoth's fierce serpents. But Naneferkaptah vanquished them, and the book was his! But Thoth was furious. "Do not allow Naneferkaptah or anyone close to him to return to his town of Memphis!" he cried to the other gods. So the gods killed the prince's wife and son. The prince was devastated and took his own life in turn. His father, the pharaoh, buried Naneferkaptah's body and the *Book of Thoth* in a secret place.

Years later another learned man, Setne, looted the book from its hidden location. Setne was then tricked into thinking that he, too, had lost everything dear to him because he stole the *Book of Thoth*. But unlike Naneferkaptah, he was given a second chance and returned the book to the tomb so that he would not be further punished. Perhaps the gods' secret knowledge was not meant for mere humans.

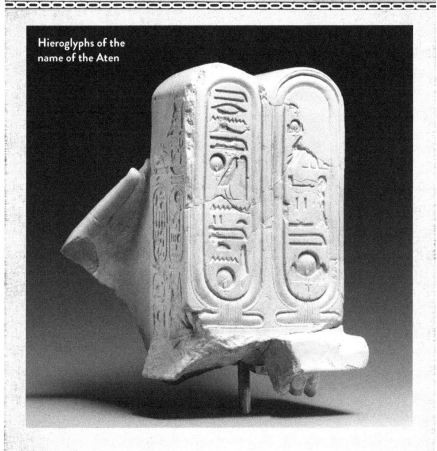

Hieroglyphs of the name of the Aten

HIEROGLYPHS

The term hieroglyphs is actually Greek for "sacred carvings." Hieroglyphs were a set of pictures used to write the ancient Egyptian language. They consisted of about 500 symbols that stood for both sounds and ideas. These signs included plants, animals, humans, pots, gods, and buildings, just to name a few—all things ancient Egyptians observed in the world around them.

SESHAT

(SECHAT)

Goddess of Scribes, Building, and Astronomy

When **Ramesses the Great**, the mighty New Kingdom pharaoh, wanted to build a god a new temple, it was an important and religious event. Stone had to be shipped down the Nile from far away. Artists and architects, and stone builders and carvers had to design and decorate. But even before any of this could happen, the king had many important religious jobs he had to do for the god. And he could not do this without the director of buildings and temples: the goddess **Seshat**.

Seshat, whose name meant "female scribe," oversaw the building of temples in Egypt. She was the daughter and associate of Thoth, and had much of his wisdom. She appeared as a woman, wearing a leopard skin over her dress and a seven-pointed star on her head. This star sat upon a long stick that came out of her headband. Around this star was a bow or a half-moon-like shape. Seshat wore a wig and held a writing tool in one hand, while in the other she sometimes held a papyrus.

Seshat was a great writer, librarian, and scholar. She and Thoth together recorded both the deeds of the pharaohs and the actions of everyday Egyptians. Seshat stood by King Ramesses and wrote down his great acts. She recorded Ramesses's journeys outside of Egypt—south to Nubia and north to Syria-Palestine—to wage war and bring back treasure. Seshat wrote down all the animals and plants the pharaoh retrieved for the gods, and all the gold and jewels. She noted how many cattle the pharaoh had in all of Egypt. She also recorded

Ramesses's jubilee—a great festival celebrating his thirtieth year ruling Egypt!

So when Ramesses came to Seshat for help constructing a new temple, she was ready. "Seshat, oh Seven-Pointed One," cried Ramesses to the wise goddess, "I need your help to lay out my new temple."

Seshat replied to Ramesses, "I have been watching you rule, and have seen all the great things you have done. I will help you build this temple, for the place you have chosen is good."

Seshat and Ramesses met at night on the land where the temple was to be built to measure out the ground plan. Temples needed to line up with the Nile and with certain stars. Seshat knew about the locations and the movements of all the stars and planets in the sky. She used her skills to plan out and measure exactly where a temple should go.

The two stood and each held a string tied to two poles. This string was pulled between them and they measured each side of the plan of the future temple while saying the proper spells and prayers. This ritual was called "stretching the cord." The four corners of the temple were chosen based on the location of four stars. They marked each corner with posts that they beat into the ground with sticks. Seshat spoke to Ramesses, "Your temple will stand firm and strong, like the sky, and it will last for as long as the earth and the gods last."

Ramesses then dug down until he reached the water below the ground. This water symbolized the new life of the temple, like the moment when Ra first made the world. Ramesses then molded bricks out of mud and straw, and placed one at each of the four corners of the temple. The bottom of the temple was filled in with more mudbricks and then sand.

Below the temple Ramesses buried a "foundation deposit," meaning rich, precious, protective, and magical goods like pottery, jewelry, amulets, tools, and objects with the king's name. These objects gave power and life to the temple and promised that no destruction would happen because of this gift to the god. Natron, or salt, was added to clean the area. Once all of these rituals were completed, it was time to start building.

The stone builders and scribes working on the temple called upon Seshat to help them. She directed them in designing the building and carving the hieroglyphs that recorded the great deeds of Ramesses. This temple would be the finest and largest Egypt had ever seen! Although she had no temple of her own, Seshat helped the kings to build all the great houses for the gods.

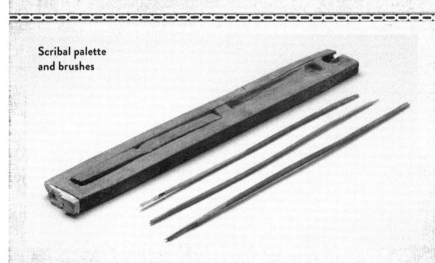

Scribal palette and brushes

SCRIBES AND WRITING

Administrators who could read and write hieroglyphs were called scribes. It is most likely that less than ten percent of the Egyptian population knew the hieroglyphic script. Scribes were often men, but there is evidence that some women, too, were taught to read and write.

BES AND TAWERET

(BISU) (TAURT, THOERIS)

God and Goddess of Home, Childbirth, Women, and Children

Weni was a typical farmer who lived his life like many Egyptians. He worked hard, growing crops and taking care of animals, and made offerings at the local temple. He, like most people in his village, was not allowed to enter certain areas of the temple. He knew little about the secret world of priests. But he, like all

Egyptians, still depended upon the gods. He prayed to them for protection and for help with his fields and family. And his favorites were the god Bes and the goddess Taweret.

Bes was a dwarf with a lion's mane and tail, and a snarl on his face. Bes always faced forward (instead of in profile, like the images of most gods and ancient Egyptians). He wore tall feathers on his head, and his legs were usually bent in a squatting or dancing position. Bes looked scary, but he was a kind and protective god to those who praised him, and was beloved by all. He safeguarded the home and the living, particularly children, mothers, and generally vulnerable individuals.

Bes's ugliness was one of his powers! He scared the evil spirits away from the house and away from his followers. Sometimes Bes carried a sword that he used to fight demons and keep out dangerous creatures.

Not only did the popular Bes protect, but he also entertained. Bes loved music and dancing, especially playing the drums and tambourine. This drum beating served two purposes: It made music that could please the gods, but it also kept the scary demons and threats away. Bes used his sword, his magic, and his loud music to keep the home and Egyptians safe.

Bes was partnered with another protective goddess—Taweret. She was a fat hippopotamus with a sagging chest, the paws of a lion, and the back of a crocodile. Taweret's name meant "the great one," and she was large and powerful. Hippopotamuses were the most dangerous animals in Egypt, and as a hippo, Taweret could choose to be violent or defensive. Usually she protected and was loved. Like wild Nile female hippos fiercely guarding their young, Taweret watched over women, children, and childbirth. Bes and Taweret were often together when new Egyptians were born, whether they were the children of the pharaoh or the children of ordinary folks like Weni.

The house Weni shared with his wife, Mery, was filled with images of Bes and Taweret. The two gods were carved into furniture legs, around mirror handles, on pottery, and on makeup jars and containers. An image of Bes was painted on the wall. Mery even had a Bes tattoo!

When Weni's wife was pregnant with their first

child, they said many offerings and prayers to Bes and Taweret. Spells were recited and rituals were performed to make sure it was a healthy and safe birth.

A woman helping with the birth brought a magical ivory wand shaped like a crescent moon to their house. The wand had carved images of Bes, Taweret, and other ferocious animal gods who held knives. The woman drew a circle in the dirt on the floor of the house around Mery with the tip of the wand. The wand created a magical space that protected Mery through childbirth with the help of these gods.

The birth was hard for Mery. A spell was said over a clay dwarf figure, and then the figure was placed upon Mery's head. Bes and Taweret watched over the birth. And when the baby was born, the two gods kept close watch over the child and mother. The wand was used again, and another circle was drawn around the tiny baby to keep away scorpions, snakes, and other dangers. Mery's baby grew up safe and healthy, under the protection of Bes and Taweret.

CHILDREN AND GAMES

Game board and pieces set up for Senet

Even with all the gods watching out for them, many ancient Egyptian children did not live to adulthood because they encountered many dangers. But they also had fun, just like children today. Children went around naked, wore their hair in a sidelock, and played outside. Sports and games were important at every age. Images remain of Egyptians wrestling, fishing, swimming, playing ball games, and practicing archery. Dice and a board game called Senet were also popular.

SOBEK

(SUCHOS, SEBEK)

God of Crocodiles and the Waters

When Horus and Seth were fighting for the office of king, Seth put a powerful substance into Horus's hands. Isis, convinced that this substance was dangerous and frightened by what she saw, cut off her son's hands. The hands fell into the Nile and sank down to the depths.

"Stay down there, hands!" Isis yelled. "You must remain separate from Horus, even if you are found again."

But Horus could not live without hands. When Horus's mother had left, Ra called out to the crocodile god, Sobek. "Sobek! Dive down and find Horus's hands!"

While his full crocodile form was common, Sobek could also have the head of a crocodile and the body of a man. On his head he wore a large sun disk crown that often included two tall feathers.

As a good crocodile, Sobek loved the Nile, and he enjoyed resting and sunning upon small islands and sandbanks, and hiding in the marshes. These were areas often difficult for travelers sailing on the river, and these people prayed to Sobek to protect them through the rocks and against the common crocodiles that hunted in the marshes. Many of Sobek's temples were built in such rocky and sandy locations along the Nile.

Sobek created the green marshes and the green crops and plants that lived along the edge of the river. He knew the Nile better than anyone. So when Ra needed someone to find Horus's hands at the bottom of the river, of course he went to Sobek.

Sobek dived down and swam through his river, searching for Horus's two hands. At last he found them.

But the hands had become living beings! They did not want to be caught, and Sobek chased them through the water.

To catch the hands, Sobek pulled up river reeds and wove a great fish trap. The hand creatures swam into the net and were caught. That is how the first fishing net was created.

Sobek pulled the captured hand creatures up to the surface. Ra took the net and put the hands in a temple where they could not cause trouble, and Isis used her magic to make her son new hands.

Sobek ruled the Nile, and all upon it and within it. He generally protected humans from the water and its creatures. But Sobek also was known to sometimes pull humans into the river, because it was his job to kill all the king's enemies who went into the Nile . . . or because he could not always control his appetite.

One day, enemies of the gods wandered into the waters of the Nile. Sobek heard them splashing and he grew angry—they should not be there! Sobek swam silently through the clear blue, as quick as his crocodile limbs could take him. He snuck up on the enemies and pounced! He ate their bodies and carried their heads back home with him.

The gods saw what Sobek had done and could not believe it. He had killed them all! "Sobek! What have you done? You must not eat their heads—spare those at least." Sobek was disappointed he could not finish his meal, but he obeyed. The gods gave Sobek some bread to make up for it, and he sadly ate the bread, wishing he could have enemy meat instead.

Sobek's hunger for meat was not just limited to humans—he also had an appetite for other gods. After Seth murdered his brother Osiris and threw his body parts all over the land and water, Sobek came across one of these limbs in the Nile. Hungry and greedy, Sobek ate the part of Osiris he found. The gods were horrified. "How could you eat part of a fellow god?" they yelled at him. To punish him, the gods cut out Sobek's tongue. And that is why crocodiles have no tongues.

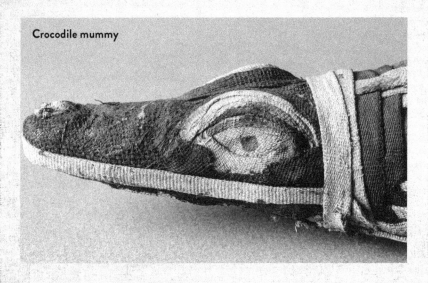
Crocodile mummy

ANIMAL MUMMIES

Egyptians mummified animals as well as humans. Some animals were believed to be the manifestation of gods; for example, some crocodiles were mummified as a form of Sobek. Cats, dogs, birds, and all types of creatures were mummified as gifts to the gods, food for the dead, or even because they had been a beloved pet.

KHNUM

(CHUNUM, KOINE, KHNEMU)

God of Potters and the Flood

Egypt was dry. The Nile flood had not come for seven years. Grain could not grow, and food was scarce. Temples were closed, and humans were desperate and fighting one another.

King Djoser, the builder of the first pyramid, did not know what to do. He asked his trusted advisor and architect, Imhotep, for help. He said, "We must bring Hapy and the Nile flood back to Egypt. Go, and look in the ancient texts for an answer to our problems. You must find where the flood comes from!"

Imhotep responded, "Yes, of course, Your Majesty!" And away he went.

Imhotep traveled to the famous sun temple at Heliopolis, where the great god Ra lived. Imhotep searched the old papyri, which very few could read, until he discovered the answer: The flood began in Elephantine.

Elephantine was an island in the southernmost part of Egypt at the first **cataract**, an area in the Nile where the rocks made sailing too difficult. Under the island there were two caverns. The Nile flood came from within these caverns, the papyrus said. So that was where Imhotep needed to go.

The island was the realm of the ram god Khnum. When Imhotep arrived, he saw Khnum, tall and imposing with a ram head, wig, double-feathered crown, and human body. Imhotep knew the river was hidden beneath the island, and he needed to find a way to set it free.

But Khnum was standing on the waters, guarding the large stone doors that kept the flood inside the caves. "Only I can open the doors to these caverns!" said Khnum. Djoser would have to make the god happy so that Khnum would open the doors. Imhotep had to learn everything he could so he could figure out what would please Khnum.

Imhotep learned the names of the gods and goddesses of Khnum's temple: Satet, Anuket, Hapy, Shu, Geb, Nut, Osiris, Horus, Isis, and Nephthys. On the island Imhotep saw tall plants and flowers. He observed the pink granite rock used for building. He saw statues and precious stones. Imhotep traveled back to King Djoser to tell him what he had learned.

Djoser was overjoyed to hear that there might be a way to make the flood return. He made offerings of bread, beer, and meat to Khnum and his gods and goddesses, and with hope, Djoser fell asleep.

Khnum came to Djoser in his dreams: "I am Khnum! I created you and all things! And I am the only one who knows how to open the door to let out the flood. Hapy and the water will flow again, the trees will be weighed down with so much fruit, and hunger will be gone!"

Djoser woke up and knew what he had to do. He made a promise to the god Khnum: "I will give the lands to the east and to the west to you, and you will have all the gifts you would like. All the good crops will come to you. All the fish and fowl caught by the fishermen and hunters will come to you. All the precious stones are yours. We will fix up your temple and it will shine."

The king was true to his word, and Khnum was pleased. The god at last opened up the stone doors, and the Nile flood came and filled the fields of Egypt once again.

The floodwaters Khnum controlled were filled with rich, black silt that gave the plants nutrients. This watery black dirt was at Khnum's command, and the god was also a great potter: He knew how to create all things with mud and clay. Khnum had a great potter's wheel. Each morning he remade the world and all within it upon this wheel. Khnum's creative abilities were powerful and influential. He created the forms of the baby gods, and the gods in turn sometimes called upon him to make the body of the god-chosen pharaoh on earth.

Khnum may have controlled the caverns of the Nile at Elephantine, but Satet, his wife, guarded all of Egypt's southern frontier. Satet wore the White Crown of Upper Egypt with two antelope horns on either side. The height of the Nile was recorded each year in Satet's temple at Elephantine. Anuket, her daughter, was also a fierce warrior. Khnum, Satet, and Anuket together formed a **triad**, a family group of three gods, who ruled from Elephantine.

NILE

As the life-giving heart of Egypt, the Nile is the longest river in the world. Flowing from south to the north, it begins in central East Africa and empties into the Mediterranean Sea. In ancient Egyptian times, the Nile flooded every summer. The flood brought water and nutrients for farming. Today, the Nile no longer floods because of the Aswan Dam, built in the 1960s.

FAMILY TREE
OF THE GODS

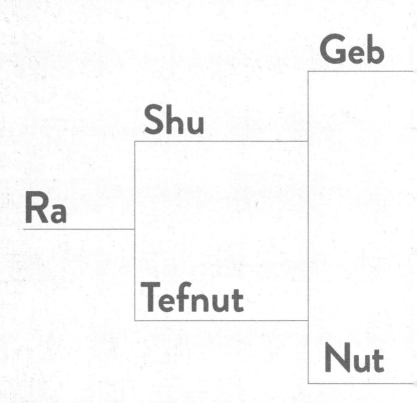

Ra

Shu

Tefnut

Geb

Nut

Isis

Horus

Osiris

Nephthys

Seth

GLOSSARY

Akhenaten: A pharaoh who, along with his queen, Nefertiti, required that all Egyptians worship a singular god called the Aten.

Ammut: The "devourer" was an underworld creature with the head of a crocodile, the mane of a lion, and the body of a hippopotamus who ate the heart of the deceased if it weighed more than the feather of Maat.

amulet: A magical and religious object that gave protection or good health and luck to its wearer, both in life and death.

Amun: A universal god whose name meant "the hidden one," he rose in popularity at the beginning of the New Kingdom (circa 1550 BCE).

Amun-Ra: A solar deity ruling over all of the earth and sky, a combination of the gods Amun and Ra.

ankh: The hieroglyph that symbolized life.

Apis Bull: The living ba and earthly messenger of the god Ptah, the Apis Bull was an oracle who could predict the future and who lived in Memphis.

Apophis: A snake god who lived in the underworld, Apophis was the enemy of Ra, the sun god, and represented chaos. The snake and Ra did battle every night.

Atef crown: Often worn by Osiris, this crown was made up of two feathers, horns, and a disk.

Aten: A form of the sun god who was especially worshipped by Akhenaten and Nefertiti, and was represented by a sun disk.

Atum: A creation god who was self-creating and whose name means "complete."

ba: One of the parts of the Egyptian soul, this was the personality or identity of an Egyptian. It often took the form of a human-headed bird.

Banebdjede: A ram-headed god from Memphis.

Byblos: A port city in modern-day Lebanon that had a strong Egyptian presence in ancient times, known for its cedarwood.

canopic jars: A set of four containers that held the lungs, stomach, intestines, and liver, which were removed from the body during mummification. These jars were usually placed in a burial near the mummy.

cataract: An area in the Nile filled with rocks and rapids where boats are unable to pass.

circa: A word that historians use to refer to approximate dates, when they do not know exactly in what year an event occurred.

crook and flail: Two scepters that represented Egyptian kingship. Osiris and the mummies of pharaohs often held them crossed over their chests.

Delta: The marshy area in northern Egypt where the Nile spreads out in multiple directions before emptying into the Mediterranean Sea.

Djoser: An Old Kingdom king whose tomb was the first pyramid—the Step Pyramid at Saqqara.

Double Crown: A crown worn by kings and deities that combined the White Crown of Upper Egypt and the Red Crown of Lower Egypt. It represented a unified Egypt.

Duat: The Egyptian underworld that existed below the earth.

Ennead: A group of gods and goddesses—usually nine. The most famous was from the city of Heliopolis.

Eye of Ra: A goddess who was the divine eye of the sun god Ra, and who often acted independently as Ra's protector or messenger. A number of goddesses could be called upon to act as the Eye of Ra.

Field of Reeds: The place in the Duat where the blessed dead lived. Egyptians traveled here after their hearts were weighed against the feather of truth, Maat.

Hall of Judgment: The place in the Duat where your heart would be weighed against the feather of truth, Maat.

Hapy: The god of the Nile, who had blue skin, a sagging chest, and a beard.

Heh: God of infinity who could also divide into eight forms, which together helped to hold up the sky.

Heliopolis: One of the locations of creation, this city was the home of Atum, Ra, and the Ennead.

hieroglyphs: A set of symbols used to write the ancient Egyptian language.

ib: The heart, which was the source of all thought and feeling, and a part of the ancient Egyptian soul.

Imhotep: One of the first named artists in history, he designed the Step Pyramid at Saqqara and was later worshiped as a god.

Isfet: The force of chaos. It was the opposite of Maat ("order") in the ancient Egyptian universe.

ka: One of the parts of the Egyptian soul, this was the life force of an ancient Egyptian. The ka could travel back and forth between the body and the person in death.

Karnak Temple: The largest temple complex surviving in Egypt. It was built in Thebes for the god Amun-Ra.

Khepri: A beetle form of the sun god Ra and the creator god Atum that pushed the morning sun across the horizon.

lotus: A Nile flower that symbolized rebirth.

Maat: The goddess of order and truth.

Memphis: The capital of Egypt during several periods of Egyptian history, located just south of modern-day Cairo.

monotheism: A religion worshipping one god. The opposite is *polytheism*, which is what the ancient Egyptians practiced.

mummiform: Having the shape of a mummy.

Mut: An Eye of Ra goddess who could take the form of a lion, popular mainly in the New Kingdom and later. She was the wife of Amun-Ra, and her temple was at Karnak.

Nefertiti: A queen who, along with her husband, Akhenaten, required that all Egyptians worship a singular god called the Aten.

Nefertum: A lion-headed god of Memphis, he was the son of Sekhmet and Ptah and often wore a lotus flower on his head.

Nekhbet: A goddess in the form of a vulture who guarded Upper Egypt. Along with Wadjet, she was one of the "two ladies."

Nile River: The longest river in the world, around which all of ancient Egyptian society was organized.

Nubia: Ancient Egypt's southern neighbor, much of which is today in northern Sudan.

Nun: The nothingness that existed before the world's creation, and the force from which all creation emerged.

oasis: A livable place with water and plants in the middle of a desert.

Opening of the Mouth ceremony: A ritual that the god Anubis performed on mummies, which gave the dead individual the ability to use their senses in the afterlife.

oracle: Someone who could see the future and provide wise counsel.

papyrus: A reed that grows in the Nile marshes. It was used as an early form of paper. The plural is *papyri*.

pharaoh: The king of ancient Egypt, who was considered to be a living god.

Ra-Atum: A combination of the gods Ra and Atum, taking the form of an old man and acting as the dying sun in the evening.

Ra-Horakhty: A form of the sun god, Ra, whose name meant "Ra who is Horus of the two horizons." Ra took this form as he traveled across the sky each day.

Ramesses the Great: Also known as Ramesses II, he was one of the most celebrated pharaohs of ancient Egypt.

Red Crown: The crown associated with Lower Egypt. Combined with the White Crown it formed the Double Crown that represented a unified Egypt.

rituals: Repeated acts performed with objects, words, or gestures within a specific time and place, often with a religious purpose.

rn: The word for "name," which for the ancient Egyptians had great and magical power, representing the person's identity.

scribe: An individual who could read and write hieroglyphs or other Egyptian scripts.

sidelock: A typical hairstyle worn by ancient Egyptian children that included a shaved head except for one long lock of hair.

sistrum: A rattle that was shaken to please and calm Egyptian gods.

sun disk: A round orb that represented the sun and sat on the heads of many ancient Egyptian deities. Ra could be represented by just a sun disk.

symbol: An object or person that stands for something else. Often it is a physical object representing an idea.

triad: A group of three gods, usually a husband, wife, and child.

Upper and Lower Egypt: Upper Egypt was the area in the south of Egypt, and Lower Egypt was in the north. At some times in history they were separate, and at times they were a unified kingdom.

Wadjet: A goddess in the form of a cobra who watched over Lower Egypt. Along with Nekhbet, she was one of the "two ladies."

wedjat eye: This eye symbolized healing and completeness, and it was part-human and part-hawk.

White Crown: The crown associated with Upper Egypt. Combined with the Red Crown it formed the Double Crown that represented a unified Egypt.

FIND OUT MORE

Want to find out more about ancient Egypt or mythology? Start here for some ways to explore further!

Books:

Everything Ancient Egypt (National Geographic Kids) by Crispin Boyer with Egyptologist James P. Allen

Treasury of Egyptian Mythology: Classic Stories of Gods, Goddesses, Monsters & Mortals (National Geographic Kids) by Donna Jo Napoli and Christina Balit

You Wouldn't Want to Be series: *An Egyptian Mummy, A Pyramid Builder*, and *Tutankhamen (Scholastic)* by various authors

Websites:

BBC History for Kids: Ancient Egypt (bbc.co.uk
/bitesize/topics/zg87xnb)
Animated videos and articles about life in ancient
Egypt.

DK Find Out: Ancient Egypt (dkfindout.com
/us/history/ancient-egypt)
Interactive encyclopedia entries about ancient Egypt
and its gods and goddesses.

NOVA: Explore Ancient Egypt (pbs.org/wgbh/nova
/ancient/explore-ancient-egypt.html)
Interactive 360-degree panoramas and photos of
ancient Egyptian temples, pyramids, and tombs.

PBS: Egypt's Golden Empire (pbs.org/empires/egypt
/index.html)
Photos, timeline, video clips, and other resources
accompanying a documentary TV series.

REFERENCES

Allen, James P. "Genesis in Egypt: The Philosophy of Ancient Egyptian Creation Accounts." Yale Egyptological Seminar, Department of Near Eastern Languages and Civilizations, Graduate School, Yale University, New Haven, CT, 1988.

Baines, John. Leonard H. Lesko, and David P. Silverman. *Religion in Ancient Egypt: Gods, Myths, and Personal Piety*. Edited by Byron E. Shafer. Ithaca: Cornell University Press, 1991.

Hart, George. *A Dictionary of Egyptian Gods & Goddesses*. New York: Routledge, 1986.

Lesoko, Barbara S. *The Great Goddesses of Egypt*. Norman: University of Oklahoma Press, 1999.

Lichtheim, Miriam. *Ancient Egyptian Literature*. Volumes 1–3. Berkeley: University of California Press, 1973.

Meeks, Dimitri, and Christine Favard-Meeks. *Daily Life of the Egyptian Gods*. Ithaca: Cornell University Press, 1996.

Pinch, Geraldine. *Egyptian Mythology: A Guide to the Gods, Goddesses, and Traditions of Ancient Egypt.* New York: Oxford University Press, 2002.

Shaw, Ian. *The Oxford History of Ancient Egypt.* Oxford: Oxford University Press, 2000.

Wilkinson, Richard H. *The Complete Gods and Goddess of Ancient Egypt.* New York: Thames & Hudson, 2017.

ACKNOWLEDGMENTS

Love and thanks to Mom, Dad, Meredith, and Lindsay for all the museum trips, proofreading, and advice. To Conor, Everly, and Alex—I can't wait until I can take you all to Egypt one day. To my Aunt Carol and Uncle John, who were the first to call me Indy, and my cousins Megan, Erin, Keith, and Craig and their families. Love and thanks to all my friends. Thanks to the Hopkins community, and special thanks to Professor Betsy Bryan and Professor Richard Jasnow for all you have taught me and continue to teach me. And finally, love and thanks to Jessie and Nefertiti, for the daily support through this process, and all the prayers to Ra.

ABOUT THE AUTHOR

 **Morgan E. Moroney** is a PhD candidate in Egyptology at Johns Hopkins University, focusing on Egyptian art and archaeology. After she received her BA from the University of Chicago, she spent five years as a book publicist in New York City before giving it all up to pursue her childhood dream of Egyptology. She has worked at several museums and excavates in Egypt and Ethiopia. She lives in Baltimore with her partner and their cat, Nefertiti. Follow her on Instagram and Twitter @Tomes_and_Tombs.

CPSIA information can be obtained
at www.ICGtesting.com
Printed in the USA
JSHW020018191020
8810JS00004BA/11